CONVICTION
AND
CIVILITY

THINKING AND COMMUNICATING CLEARLY
ABOUT WHAT THE BIBLE TEACHES

BOBBY HARRINGTON & JASON HENDERSON

CONTENTS

RENEW

RENEWING THE TEACHINGS OF JESUS
TO FUEL DISCIPLE MAKING

RENEW.ORG

CHAPTER 1

Convicted Civility

I (Bobby) thought that it was an ideal summer night. I was attending an event for Christian leaders, and the evening was perfect for an engaging conversation outside. Dallas Willard had just made a presentation to a group of scholars and seminary students. We were all relaxing after dinner out on the patio, and the conversation was as pleasant and clear as the evening air. Dallas was an intellectual giant of the faith and a philosophy professor at the University of Southern California, uniquely respected by many secular and Christian leaders. This circumstance gave me a chance to ask Dallas a question, one that I had wanted to ask for ten years—it was about the nature of saving faith.

I worded the question in such a way that many people could have been offended, but I couldn't think of a different way to ask it. Dallas listened to me, then responded in a kind and gentle way. He restated the question to make sure that he understood it. Then carefully, yet succinctly, he described the different ways by which people have sought to answer my question and the nuances involved. Then, he clarified the exact nature of my question in a slightly different way to make sure that he fully understood the motivation for it. He then answered the question calmly and with a kind, yet factual manner. After that, the conversation moved on to another topic.

Neither the question nor the answer impacted me as much as the demeanor and the approach that Willard demonstrated while answering. It demonstrated a cluster of important elements that reflected wisdom, love, critical thinking, and nuance… and all of those things in a five-minute conversation. Just after he died, Willard's daughter published a book that Willard had not quite finished at the time of his death. The title reflects his approach to my question that night: *The Allure of Gentleness: Defending the Faith in the Manner of Jesus.*[1]

In this book, Dallas Willard summarizes the approach we are going to recommend to you this way: "The means of our communication needs to be gentle, because gentleness also characterizes the subject of our communication. What we are seeking to defend or explain is Jesus himself, who is a gentle, loving shepherd. If we are not gentle in how we present the good news, how will people encounter the gentle and loving Messiah we want to point to?"[2]

When I reflect on that evening, four elements stand out about the way in which Willard handled that difficult conversation. We feel these elements mirror the approach described in Jesus' teaching: 1) convicted civility, 2) a relational basis for conversations, 3) critical thinking, and 4) the nuance of knowing that things can be black and white… or grey.

The first of these is a term that Richard J. Mouw called "convicted civility" in his book *Uncommon Decency.*[3] This is the posture we want to strike when approaching these crucial conversations. We live in a time where we must learn when and how to communicate without eliciting extreme and polarized reactions as in the opening example.

Mouw does not suggest our problems will go away simply by being more civil. Convicted civility is more than a simple outward show of politeness. In fact, Mouw quotes journalist Martin Marty who observed, "The people who are good at being civil often lack strong convictions and people who have strong convictions often lack civility."[4] Mouw states that simple civility can be a form of hypocrisy, hiding hostile feelings behind a mask. A richer posture of true "inner" civility is what we are after. This involves the development of heartfelt commitment to others and to the wellbeing of even those you seriously disagree with. Sounds a bit like Jesus, doesn't it? Mouw describes a state of "passionate intensity" where one can remain convicted, driving toward truth, and combine it with a civil outlook. In fact, Mouw says, inner civility can help us become more mature Christians and may increase, instead of decrease, conviction.[5]

How do we develop this inner state of passionate politeness?

My wife and I (Jason) have two children. As parents, we have found more than one situation where we disapprove of how one of the kids is treating their sibling. We will say something like, "Be kind!" or, "Stop being selfish!" When one considers these commands outside of the moment, it becomes easy to see the absurdity of that ask. We may as well say, "Stop acting like children!" Instead, we need to patiently and consistently coach them to develop the inner desire to treat each other well. The same principle applies with internalizing civility. It takes work and time to develop. One does not suddenly decide to "turn on" this approach and commitment to others.

An approach of convicted civility, for a Christian, should begin with how we present ourselves to others. We are called to be Christlike, which means that we reflect the kindness and gentleness of God. It will lend credibility and legitimacy to your conversation if you have established yourself as a reputable agent of God's righteousness. This by no means implies you must be perfect, but an honest attempt at public righteousness will make the message more credible as we have a "legitimate" invite for others to be more like us.[6]

Mouw outlines the practical attitudes that one can develop to present this posture of civility when encountering those different from us. *Empathy* is the first. This is sometimes analogized as "walking in another's shoes" or "sitting in their seat." Mouw describes this approach as reducing psychological distance[7] between you and another. He describes empathy as developing a "want" to learn about others. By becoming familiar with the experience of those different from us, we reduce our self-centeredness and come closer to God's purpose for us.[8]

The next attitude Mouw mentions—one that will enhance the attitude of empathy—is a good dose of *curiosity.* Developing a healthy desire to better understand the world God has created, including the beliefs of the beings he created in it, will help us step out of our own understandings and discover the "whys" of others.[9] If you want to help someone by adding or changing an idea they currently hold, it makes sense that you explore what ideas are there already and how they got there.

Muow delves into a third aspect of convicted civility, which is an attitude of being *teachable.*[10] This could be described as the humble acknowledgement that we can all learn from one another.

We must maintain a humble posture that assumes no matter what opinions we hold, those opposing our views may have lessons for us also. He underlines his point this way: "No matter how antagonistic a perspective may be toward things we hold precious, we should be at least willing to listen… God often instructs believers in unpredictable ways. The prophet Balaam was corrected by words that came from the mouth of his donkey. A group of pagan sailors confronted Jonah with the fact that he was trying to run from the call of God…. The Lord often sends teachers our way. We need to be open to the lessons he wants us to learn from them."[11] Despite any judgment of others' ideas, right or wrong, you can learn from the dialogue you share.

CHAPTER 2

The Problem Today

Lee Strobel's book, *The Case for Faith,* includes an analogy offered by Dr. Peter Kreeft to describe difficulty in communications and understanding.[12] A hunter happens upon a bear caught in a trap. The hunter, out of sympathy, wants to set the bear free. He tries everything he can with food and a soothing voice, but he can't set the bear free. In order to help the bear, the hunter must subdue the animal either by force or with drugs. Additionally, the hunter finds he must push the bear's leg a bit deeper into the trap to release the mechanism to open the trap's jaws and free the bear. The bear, of course, does not understand that any of this is being done out of compassion; rather, he thinks the hunter is trying to hurt or possibly kill him. The bear would be convinced the hunter is his enemy who is trying to cause him suffering and pain. He would be wrong, reaching the incorrect conclusion because he is not a human being.

This analogy might resemble the relationship between someone trying to share Jesus' teachings in today's culture and those unwilling to give these teachings, especially on difficult topics, a fair hearing. There is a similar resistance and communications gap when trying to express the compassion behind some of Jesus' more counter-cultural ideas. The one sharing the truth of Scripture is bringing a life-giving message, one that will save and bring peace and freedom. To the listener it can sound narrow and culturally offensive. They may tune it out or become belligerent if it is not handled very carefully and with an approach like the one we described above.

The Barna group reported that two out of five Americans believe "religion" and "people of faith" are part of the problems of our country.[13] Also, only one-fifth of American adults believe clergy are a credible source of wisdom.[14] It would seem a prevailing attitude of "the bear" is present as we approach others in an attempt to share biblical truth. It follows that when it comes to hard issues the trend is, at best, a prevailing attitude that religion is not something worth paying attention to and, at worst, bigoted extremism. Mainstream culture has become such a dominant influence that it forces itself as popular and true on anyone unwilling to challenge it.

In today's popular social mediums for communication the challenge of being heard and understood is compounded. You've been there haven't you? You post something on an impulse, only to realize… maybe you shouldn't have.

Within twenty-four hours, dozens of people have replied to your post. Surely these are "likes" and affirmations from the supporters of common sense… wait-what?!? How did we end up in a virtual shouting match and why do you now own a string of dialogue that includes language you wouldn't want your friends and family to read?

A Cornell University study which tracked online social media debates[15] found that in more than 70 percent of these back-and-forth dialogues no one was persuaded away from their original point of view. When someone *was* persuaded, one of the top correlative reasons was group response. In other words, an individual's opinion yielded to the most popular response if enough people expressed it. *Inc. Magazine* quoted another study that helps explain the reason these online conversations spin out of control so quickly, and it is no surprise.[16] We respond differently to what people write as opposed to what they say—even if those things are exactly the same.

Research suggests the best way for people to discuss differences is by talking to each other. But that may not seem easy and presents its own requirements in order to gain a true hearing. How then do we approach those seeking the truth in a world that often thinks biblical truth is irrational and irrelevant? Further, how do we tackle hard topics with those who don't yet share our worldview because it has such high potential for alienation or social ridicule or both? While it requires a measure of risk-taking and "sticking your neck out," many are willing to engage with you if you approach things well. Then how do we handle these engagements with those who offer openings into discourse or even debate?

In this short book, we present a path of engagement based on two key perspectives. First is the path of convicted civility. We believe that people will be willing to listen to what we say if we present our ideas in a civil and relational manner while communicating convictions in a substantive and nuanced way.

The second perspective is theological. People get easily upset at both a cognitive and emotional level if they believe they are being asked to accept every doctrine as essential for one's faith or if their thinking is not clear about the stakes involved in a particular biblical element. People can also become rattled in conversations when they are fuzzy on the different types of truths that are found in the Bible. We believe there is a need to clarify that some elements of biblical teaching are essential, others are important, and a few are personal. A clear delineation of these elements of the faith will give you the ability to engage with both courage and sensitivity. How does that work? We will find out in the next chapter.

CHAPTER 3

Remember the Relationship

We are surrounded by a culture that is quickly moving toward isolationism. Screens and social media are taking the place of face-to-face relationship building. It's complicated further because the relationships we do create are usually only with people who are similar to us. Take this statistic, for example: only 17 percent of Americans say they enjoy spending time with people who are *not like themselves*.[17] As a way to quickly think about your relational circle, try this experiment: pick up your phone and look at the last ten texts and phone calls. Chances are high that most of them are to and from those who look like you, think like you, and worship like you. Chris Heuertz is a Christian author who was mentored by Mother Teresa. He says this lack of relational diversity keeps us poor in friendship while maintaining a belief that there is an *us and them*, rather than a *we*. Heuertz says it is only through relationships with others that we can become the "we" Christ intends the church to be.[18]

As we strive to be more like Jesus we must go out of our way to engage those different from us. We must develop the empathy, curiosity, and humility we discussed in the last chapter to do this. As we understand others' perspectives better, we can begin to move toward them easier. We can begin to relate and increase our care for them. People listen to those who care about them.

As we develop these skills and move toward others, relationships will be created and strengthened. Strong relationships are the foundation needed to work through the nuances of biblical truth. Likewise, discipleship is best done relationally. Therefore, if relationships are, in part, a way the Holy Spirit delivers saving grace, we should treat relationships as sacred.

Let's be clear: we love others not just to help them but also to emulate Jesus and obey God (1 John 3:16). When we are like Jesus, love becomes the hallmark of our relationship with others (John 3:16). We relate to people with the same kind of love that God has poured out on us (Rom. 5:5). We like to put it this way: Jesus-like love is the foundation and the fruit of true Christian engagement. 1 John 3:14 puts it well: "We know that we have passed from death to life, because we love each other. Anyone who does not love remains in death." The way we describe it at Renew is that we are sold out on relational discipleship. Relational discipleship begins with hello. That means we believe the best context for sharing biblical truth is a life-on-life relationship.

In *The Disciple Maker's Handbook,* I (Bobby) and my writing partner Josh Patrick emphasize the importance that relationship plays in discussing Jesus' teachings. We describe it this way:

> In the context of personal relationships, questions can be asked, real-life stories can be shared, sin can be confessed, accountability can be offered, and encouragement can be given. There is a greater capacity for truth transfer. Coincidentally, this describes how Jesus made his own disciples. Jesus' ministry teaches us that disciple making is a relational process, one built on trust.[19]

We build relationships wherever we can because we know that truth travels best when it is shared between friends. What does this relational dynamic look like? Where does it begin? In *Good Faith*, Gabe Lyons suggests a starting point of *listening*. Show the person you are dialoguing with that you care about what they think and why they have come to these conclusions; show them you respect their intellectual process.[20] This sounds a little bit like an attitude of empathy and curiosity. Lyons, in an interview about his book, added that humility in these conversations "is critical." We should go into the conversation recognizing that we can learn something and emphasize points of agreement.[21]

Again, to emphasize the point: remembering the relationship is another way of expressing the Great Commandment in practice: loving God and loving others. That is what Jesus did for his disciples and it is what Jesus tells us to do in John 13:34 when he tells us: "A new command I give you: Love one another. As I have loved you, so you must love one another" (John 13:34).

There is an example of cultivating this type of relationship in *The Disciple Maker's Handbook*. It is the story of a small group of men that bonded through a series of meetings.[22] Josh Patrick started the group, and it has since continued on with new members as the original members were released to start groups of their own. I (Jason) can witness to this story first hand; I was a part of the first group described.

I remember that the group felt a little bit like a formal process at first, awkward and rote. Eventually, through repeated meeting and sharing, the miracle of relational discipleship occurred. It took investment, not just by the leader but also by each member of the relational group, and it took intentionality. We promote this intentional approach to Jesus-like love. Investing intentionally and engaging relationally and transparently with others, even those (perhaps especially those) that are different from us.

CHAPTER 4

Hone Your Critical Thinking

A Pharisee asked Jesus, "Teacher, which is the greatest commandment in the Law?" He answered, "You shall love the Lord your God with all your heart and with all your soul and with all your mind. This is the first and greatest commandment."[23] As John Piper wrote in *Think: The Life of the Mind and the Love of God*:

> Jesus says to do this not only with our heart and soul but also with our mind.... What does it mean to love God 'with all your mind'? I take it to mean that we direct our thinking in a certain way; namely, our thinking should be wholly engaged to do all it can to awaken and express the heartfelt fullness of treasuring God above all things.[24]

We will be faced with many questions about Jesus and the Bible. Our knowledge of Scripture will help us, but most of this "answering" is simply scratching intellectual itches.

We need to dig beyond the simple curiosity. We have never seen someone come to salvation because of a clever answer to a biblical riddle. The spiritually curious usually have a deeper motivation. Seek the motivations behind the person's question, and you may find they are asking you to help them. This requires ministering to a person's true needs and will almost always point to Jesus as an answer. At the core, usually people have two big asks: 1) "Is there a God?" and 2) if so, "Does he care about me?"

The hunter and bear analogy we mentioned above is helpful and clever, but it doesn't perfectly apply at all times. Not only is there an intellectual perspective gap making it hard to comprehend the actions (or inaction) of God and the teachings of Jesus, but there is also an emotional heart-struggle to trust his love through pain or in the face of deafening cultural messages. Many you will encounter will desire answers and evidence that correspond to their experience. If the only reasoning offered is "just accept this on faith," they'll assume that religion is not for "the thinkers."

Critical thinking requires reasoning. We are commanded to give "reason for the hope" we have to others.[25] And it needs to be a thoughtful reason that relates to the real world. It needs to be a reason that explains questions about Christianity, and that means working out those explanations to questions in advance of them being asked. Be prepared to explain your positions on hard topics. You don't need all the answers, but you need some. We have a uniqueness in Christ that elevates our worldview.

Every person engaged in discipleship is a theologian. Whenever we think or speak about God we are engaging in theological activity. Therefore, critical thinking is an essential element of discipleship. Let us say it again: *everybody is a theologian.* Civility, kindness, and authentic interest in others wins a hearing, but we must accept the mantle of being good thinkers and responsible theologians. We must have clear thoughts and arguments. We do this for ourselves, as people who want to get things right, and we also do it for others. If our listeners suspect there is a lack of substance to our worldview, they will check out of the conversation, no matter how friendly.

Generations may change, but this element of approaching others doesn't. Ravi Zacharias in an interview with *Tabletalk Magazine* put it this way:

> Our youth know firsthand what the world has to offer. They need to be reached at a younger age because of the world of the Internet that ravages young minds sooner than ever before. Building their faith is not a prime strength in our churches today. We seem to think that we need to entertain them into the church. But what you win them with is often what you win them to. They can see through a hollow faith in a hurry. Their minds are hungry for coherence and meaning. They long to think things through. They long to know why the gospel is both true and exclusive.[26]

CHAPTER 5

Everything is Black and White... or Grey

We are in a new day in terms of how people think in our Western culture. The old way, called "the modern world," overstated how much could be known about God, religion, and morality. Put simply: people overstated the truth that could be known.

We now live in a different time. Many are skeptical about our ability to know truth at all. The new way, the post-modern philosophical framework, understates how much can be known. Put simply: all truth claims are suspect, everyone is biased, and truth (especially religious truth) is un-knowable.

The Oxford Dictionary chose "post-truth" as the 2016 word of the year. *The Washington Post* released this news by saying, "It's official: Truth is dead. Facts are passe."[27] They point out that the dictionary defines "post-truth" as "relating to or denoting circumstances in which objective facts are less influential in shaping public opinion than appeals to emotion and personal belief." This way of viewing life presents many problems for us all. The resultant problems can be acute for Christians.

We must start by acknowledging that in the past, churches and church leaders often overstated what could be known. I

(Bobby) studied under Thomas Oden, who did a lot of scholarly work describing the influence of modern thinking on Christians from the French Revolution of 1789 to the fall of the Berlin Wall in 1989. He says that this period was characterized by an over-optimism in our ability to objectively know the truth. Many fundamentalist Christian denominations in North America were founded in this time, and their identity was often based upon finding one or two *unique truths*. They were so sure about these truths that they could claim that they alone were the "right church," because they uniquely practiced their one or two unique truths.

The assumptions of the modern world no longer work for people. They were unrealistic and overrated. In some circles, many people no longer believe that truth of any kind can even be truly known. Again, there is something important to emphasize. In the hard sciences like math or chemistry or engineering or medicine, many people still believe that objective truth is knowable. But the skeptical framework is especially dominant when it comes to moral, religious, and political issues. Feelings are more important than facts in these realms. The new ideal is to hold to individual truth, and that is different from someone else's truth. We are all supposed to respect everyone's feelings, to respect everyone's unique truth. In these areas, most hold to the belief that all truth is relative.

Many older Christians need to admit to this point: there have been a lot of overstated things in conservative Christian circles. And over-statement is often coupled with legalism and judgment. It is true, some things are relative and we should not have a hard time admitting this fact. But that does not mean that everything is relative. When we believe that all truth is relative, it leads to chaos.

This also naturally leads to self-inspired theology. Many people just come up with their own ideas about God and the truths of Scripture. Then they treat them as truth—truth that is equal to anyone else's truth. Our society champions the reality that not everything is black or white.

We believe there is a better way of thinking and knowing. We can recommend certain philosophers for those who want to go deeper, but for this paper, let's keep it basic.[28] Here is a common-sense approach to how we know certain moral or religious truths. We want to ask people to acknowledge certain clear truths. Except for sociopaths, there is common moral knowledge, even if it is often overstated.

Here are three absolute factual truths from everyday life:

- Water boils at 100°C (or 212°F) in Chicago.
- Antibiotics kill certain bacteria.
- An apple is not an orange.

Here are three moral truths that most agree are absolute:

- It is wrong to sexually molest small children.
- It is wrong to murder someone.
- It is wrong to steal what is not yours.

Here are some examples of statements which include things that are grey:

- Men and women sometimes see the same thing differently.
- People from different cultures and different ethnicities can see certain truths differently.
- Sincere and morally good Christians can hold different religious positions.

If we take this common-sense approach to the "truths of life," we can also use it to help us with elements of truth as we approach the Bible.

We do not have time in a short book like this to delve into the issues of how we know what we know (epistemology), but we are comfortable appealing to common sense for the vast majority of people. We hope that our examples make the point—no one is truly a relativist. We also think the whole conversation is vitally important because too much of the Western Christianity that we have inherited was built around overstating truths that were not essential or vitally important for the faith (as we address below).

Here are four key postures that we recommend because they are based on applying the same common-sense approach to the Bible.

1. Truth is Knowable, but Often Complex.

Knowing the truth is often hard and confusing.[29] But in most areas of life we know that if we are careful, if we examine all the evidence, and if we use good reasoning, then we can find a lot of truth. We want to be "authentic and careful" truth seekers. It is important to take the same approach as we examine the Bible. The Apostle Paul demonstrated this; he regularly reasoned with people about the truths of Jesus (Acts 17:2, 17; 18:4, 19). The Bible itself commends those who study the Bible to seek God's truth.

We also point to the Bereans as good historical examples of those seeking to know truth. They were different than other people with whom the Apostle Paul shared God's truth. The Bible describes how they investigated what Paul was teaching: "Now the Berean Jews were of more noble character than those in Thessalonica, for they received the message with great eagerness and examined the Scriptures every day to see if what Paul said was true" (Acts 17:11).

2. Jesus Provides Holistic Authentication of His Truth.

The Bible shows us that we can know the truth of Jesus in a multifaceted, holistic way. We look to facts, history, intuition, Scripture, obedience, community—and especially the inner promptings of the Holy Spirit—as important guides. In the pursuit of truth these should not be in conflict with each other; they should reflect harmony. If we focus on just one part we will truncate our ability to know the truth about Jesus. God wants us to love him with "all of [our] heart, mind, soul, and strength" (Luke 10:27), and relying on our "heart, mind, soul, and strength" is also how we best come to know his truth.

3. Focus on the Clear and Central Truths.

When it comes to life, some things are clearer and more central than others. Almost everyone says that morally, "murder is wrong," "physical child abuse is wrong," and "the starving children must be fed." And certain truths in science are clear and foundational (see the examples above). Likewise, those seeking to know the truth about Jesus will do best when they ask about the things made clear and central in the Bible: "Jesus' death, burial, and resurrection," "The forgiveness of sins," and "What it means to love like Jesus." Christianity, like common morals and science, is much easier to evaluate this way.

4. Listen to the Classic and Historical Christian Consensus

People have been following Jesus for about 2,000 years in all kinds of contexts, cultures, and countries. That is a lot of Christians to have come before us. They have been led by the Holy Spirit and they uniformly came to a classic and historical consensus on certain truths that have stood the test of time. They are not perfect guides, but those Christians who have gone before us have something to show us. As an example, imagine you are with 100 people who have thought a lot about something, and after a lot of thought, prayer, and study 98 believe one way. Then, a newcomer arrives and thinks differently. It is wise to listen carefully to the 98. Likewise, if we are thinking so differently than all of those Christians who have come before us we should carefully ask, "Is it the Holy Spirit speaking to us or is it a pressure to conform to culture?"

If the modern world overstated truth, the post-modern world tends to understate truth. We have a crisis of epistemology—of knowing what we know. But reflection on human experience with some common-sense background from everyday life can show us the way forward, even as we approach things with humility.

Not everything is grey. Black is still black, not white. While many things are relative, there are still absolute truths and truths that, with good reasoning, become clearer and clearer. In the next chapter we want to introduce you to a model of truth that will pull these learnings together. This model helps us to see what is black and white—and what different shades of grey may look like when we study the Bible.

CHAPTER 6

Three Elements of Biblical Teaching

Many people are confused about the teachings of Jesus in the Bible. They do not know how to discern what is essential from what is non-essential. There is an old statement coming out of the Protestant Reformation that many people embraced: in essentials, unity; in opinions, liberty; in all things, love.[30] It was a very helpful statement for many people. But it always contained within itself an unresolved problem: what about the items that are neither essential nor a matter of opinion? Furthermore, what makes a doctrine essential? Could it be that what is essential for one person might be non-essential for another?

We want to introduce you to a paradigm that is uniquely promoted through Renew. We know many others who independently came to this same paradigm or one similar to it. But we promote it because we find that this model helps us to take all biblical truth seriously and enables us to focus on the essential and important elements of the faith, without getting caught up in divisive things. The following summary paragraph was composed and agreed upon after in-depth prayer, reflection and discussion by Renew leaders:

Essential, Important and Personal Elements: We believe the Scriptures reveal three distinct elements of the faith: *essential* elements which are necessary for salvation; *important* elements which are to be pursued so that we faithfully follow Christ; and *personal* elements or opinion. The gospel is *essential.* Every person who is indwelt and sealed by God's Holy Spirit because of their faith in the gospel is a brother or a sister. *Important* but secondary elements of the faith are vital. Our faithfulness to God requires us to seek and pursue them, even as we acknowledge that our salvation may not be dependent on getting them right. And third, there are personal matters of opinion, disputable areas where God gives us personal freedom. But we are never at liberty to express our freedom in a way that causes others to stumble in sin. In all things, we want to show understanding, kindness, and love.

We think this three-tier model is very helpful and biblical. The first and most fundamental task is to wrap our minds around what is essential to the faith. Jesus and his gospel—and our response of faith—is what is essential. We want to champion and be uncompromising on these things.

We must face the challenge of tolerance here full force. Many Christians want to embrace the spirit of our age and be tolerant, saying any belief in Jesus is good enough. Sometimes they will say, "The Jesus of Mormonism, the Jesus of the Koran, and the Jesus of the Bible are all the same." That cannot be true. The Jesus of Mormonism is the blood brother of Satan and he is only one god among billions of gods in the universe. And the Jesus of the Koran is not the Son of God, and he did not die on the cross for our sins. So, if it is just Jesus, then which Jesus are we talking about? We must get things right at this level—these are heaven and hell issues.

There are secondary but important teachings to identify, too. This can be threatening. Just recently, I (Bobby) had a young lady who joined the small group my wife and I lead. In our small group, made of people in their 30s, we talked about various topics from week to week. An issue came up that bothered Janice, one of the people in our group (not her real name). Janice reached out and wanted to know the position of the church on a particular doctrine. I sent the church's position paper to her. When I and another woman (who discipled women in the group) talked with her, Janice revealed that she had started to read the paper but had stopped because she disagreed with it. She said that she disagreed with it so much that she was anxious for several days. This made her not want to have a conversation. Instead, she no longer wanted to attend the church because of what the church believed on this particular issue.

I knew this was an important (even if non-essential) doctrine, so it was important to have a conversation with Janice. So, I asked her to sit down and talk, but she wouldn't. Even though it was a non-essential doctrine, Janice treated it like it was essential for her. In her fear of dealing with the issue, she would not even study it simply because she had never heard anyone teach that doctrine before. It is a reminder of how hard it can be to look at and discuss some topics—especially when the category of important elements is misunderstood.

Pete Scazzero is an expert on disciple-making relationships and emotional health. He tells his own story of how he was trying to disciple people but did not make much progress until he started to deal with his emotional health, as well as his wife's and his church's health. Since then, things have radically changed for the better in his family and in the church that he leads. Pete has written many books on emotionally healthy churches, leadership, and discipleship.[31] We tell you about Pete and his teachings on emotional health and emotional reactions because we have found that what he describes is often true, and they have big impact on how people are affected by diversity in doctrine.

Peter helps us to see that if people do not have clear thinking about the stakes of different doctrines, they can overreact. So, one of the keys to an emotionally healthy spirituality and to healthy reactions to diversity of doctrine is clear thinking. When we know the category into which a doctrine or practice fits, we know how to properly assess its seriousness and when it is (or is not) a threat to the faith God tells us to uphold (Jude 3; 1 Cor. 15; etc.).

Most doctrines are important or personal. Few are essential, but the essential doctrines are foundational. They will literally determine where people will spend eternity. We should get upset about compromises to the faith at this level. Even the Apostle Paul, as Galatians describes, gets very upset because the Galatians are compromising on the Gospel. If you read Galatians 1:6-10, you can almost hear Paul's strong reaction:

> I am astonished that you are so quickly deserting the one who called you to live in the grace of Christ and are turning to a different gospel— which is really no gospel at all. Evidently some people are throwing you into confusion and are trying to pervert the gospel of Christ. But even if we or an angel from heaven should preach a gospel other than the one we preached to you, let them be under God's curse! As we have already said, so now I say again: If anybody is preaching to you a gospel other than what you accepted, let them be under God's curse! Am I now trying to win the approval of human beings, or of God? Or am I trying to please people? If I were still trying to please people, I would not be a servant of Christ.

The gospel is a serious doctrine in the Bible. Paul's emotional tone corresponds to his words. He is astonished and alarmed.

Our model emphasizes three elements of faith. Some are essential elements, some are important elements, and some are personal elements. We believe a healthy theology of delineating between these three elements can aid us in having conversations that are less threatening. It can help us to focus on being disciples and making disciples without getting side tracked by overly fixating on doctrine.

Think of concentric circles with core truths in the middle, and moving outward, the truths become more personal.[32] Here is a diagram that will help you envision what we are describing:

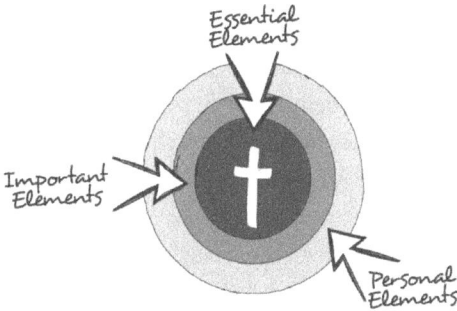

Jim Putman is a good friend of mine (Bobby's). We have had many conversations over many topics for many years. In the words of Jim, "We like to get in the ring and have hard talks about the teachings of God's Word." We can argue hard and be okay with a difficult discussion because we both have a clear understanding of the boundaries on different doctrinal levels in the Bible. We also have a great relationship and love each other as brothers.

Recently, Jim and his son, Christian, joined me on a trip to Israel. It was funny because on the trip, Jim and I had enough "hard conversations" that some people with us were amazed how we could get down into serious debates, resolve them, and keep enjoying our time together. But that is the beauty of the biblical model of dialogue, what we're calling "conviction and civility." Jim and I know the stakes in our debates and we sharpen each other through these conversations like "iron sharpening iron" (Prov. 27:17).

On this same trip to Israel, I also learned how Jim had taken this model and adapted it to Real Life Ministries, the church where he serves as Lead Pastor. The way they translate it for their context in northern Idaho has been helpful for them. It is the same concept but a different analogy. The most amusing part of all this was how I learned about their application of the model.

Jim's son, Christian, is a student minister. We were talking about student ministry on the bus in Israel—a great conversation. In the midst of the conversation, Christian wanted to tell me about how they teach their junior high and high school students to understand doctrine. He explained the model to me like I had never heard it before. All the while, I was smiling because I was proud of him.

Christian called it the "Three Buckets Model." He said to me, "Bobby, you might find this helpful because it really helps our students. We teach them that doctrine fits into three buckets." Then he asked me to envision three nested buckets like this picture shows:[33]

From a distance, it might look like there is just one bucket here. That is how people can look at the Bible. *Everything is of equal importance*, they think. But it's not. There are different layers, different categories, and different levels of importance. We can think of issues as though they fit into one of three "buckets":

Christian went on to explain the buckets to me: "First bucket issues are essential, second bucket issues are important, and third bucket issues are personal." I was *really* smiling at this point. I had never heard anyone put it quite like this. Jim had worked with Christian (and other leaders at their church), and they took the perspective we had hammered out years before, adapted it for their cultural context, and made it practical and easy to understand for their people.

Jason and I believe this model may help to simplify what we're talking about here. It may also be easier for some readers or those you know—especially teens—to discern a topic's category. In order to do this, we can ask ourselves of whatever issue we're considering: *Which bucket does this particular issue fit inside?*

In the next chapter, we want to get down, even more, into the specifics of this topic of "the buckets," but as we close this chapter, we want to reiterate one point. Many of us need help with clear thinking on what is at stake in disagreements. Some things are not as important as we might think or feel they are; other things should be more important to us than we might realize at first. Join us as we consider how to make this way of approaching biblical truth practical for you.

CHAPTER 7

Essential Elements: The First Bucket

The essential and central issues in the Bible have to do with Jesus Christ, first and foremost. John 14:6 teaches us that Jesus "is the way, the truth and the life." The greatest reality in the Bible is that God sent Jesus Christ into the world to save us out of Satan's dark kingdom, transfer us into Jesus' kingdom, transform us in this life, and take us to the new heaven and new earth so that we can enjoy an eternal relationship with him forever in the next life (Col. 1:13-14; John 3:16).

Essential truth is bedrock, foundational truth. The gospel and our faith response to Jesus' gospel are essential truths. The Bible says that we enter Jesus' kingdom when we turn from our sinful ways to place our faith in Jesus Christ. Here is our summary of the gospel (Rom. 1:16-17; 1 Cor. 15:1-8; 2 Tim. 2:8; etc.):

> The Good News is that God sent his one and only Son, Jesus the Messiah, to save us. Jesus became one of us, taught us how to live, and then…

- He died on the cross for our sins.
- He was buried.
- He rose on the third day, according to the Scriptures, and appeared to many witnesses.
- He ascended into heaven and sent his Spirit.
- Jesus has been enthroned as King of Kings and Lord of Lords.
- He is coming back to *judge the living and the dead.*
- But first, he invites everyone into his kingdom, where, by this gospel of grace, we are forgiven, made blameless, and empowered for a new life in this world and in the next.

> We respond to the gospel by faith, which means we trust and follow Jesus as his disciples in all things.[34]

Those who accept and commit themselves to Jesus and his gospel become disciples. Notice an essential element is our response to the gospel—we must respond with faith.

The Bible teaches that genuine, saving faith is more than mere intellectual agreement or simply emotional warmth toward God; it is living and active. Faith is surrendering our self-rule to God's rule through Jesus by the power of the Spirit. We surrender by trusting and following Jesus as both Savior and Lord in all things. Faith includes repentance, allegiance, loyalty, and faithfulness to him.[35] We summarize the nature of saving faith by saying that it means we trust and follow Jesus as his disciples. By this kind of faith, we become true disciples—people who follow

Christ, are changed by him, and join his kingdom mission (Matt. 4:19).[36]

There is so much that we could say about these essential elements. But we must state this clearly: "The gospel is the Good News—the best and most important announcement that anyone could ever hear."[37] Consider these things:

- This gospel is the central message of the Holy Scriptures and the key to understanding them.[38]
- This gospel focuses on Jesus Christ, his person, his redemptive work on the cross, and his launching of the kingdom of God.
- This gospel declares that the only way to know God is through Jesus Christ and his reconciling work on the cross.
- This gospel proclaims Jesus Christ as the living savior, king, teacher, life, and hope of all who put their trust in him. It tells us that the eternal destiny of all people depends on whether or not they are in right standing with God through Christ.

The gospel is so simple that small children can understand it, yet so profound that the wisest theologians will never exhaust its riches.

When we teach on these items, we carefully look at Scripture (there are ninety-two references to *the gospel* in the New Testament, with 1 Corinthians 15:1-8 and Galatians 1:6-10 being prominent among them). We may also find the Apostle's Creed to be helpful because it correlates to the gospel. It is the earliest Christians' statement of faith outside the Bible. It was defined a long time ago by those who lived close in time to the apostles, and it has stood the test of time.[39]

We have to be straightforward and candid at this point. Here are some teachings that are common but should cause concern.

The reason for concern is they are out of step with the teaching of the gospel. You will hear people say things like the following:

- "We are saved by being good people, whether or not you believe in Jesus."
- "People will be saved in other religions—they teach the same thing."
- "Muslims and Mormons believe in the same Jesus we believe in."
- "The Roman Catholic Church teaches the same thing about the gospel and salvation as Bible-believing evangelicals, even with doctrines like purgatory."

These are just samples of areas where different faiths *do not teach* the same gospel.[40] There are many cults and other groups that do this, too. Jesus and the gospel are sacred to those who follow the Bible. It must be important enough to us that we will state it and defend it from error.

Saving faith is also essential. It is the necessary response to Jesus and the gospel. Ephesians 2:8-9 puts it succinctly: "For it is by grace you have been saved, through faith—and this is not from yourselves, it is the gift of God." The gospel of grace is God's part. Faith is our part.

As a careful study of the Bible reveals, saving faith is not simply trust or mental assent; it is also active and obedient. Saving faith must be expressed in a life of discipleship: active obedience and the pursuit of God through Jesus. The second chapter of James states it succinctly:

- "You believe that there is one God. Good! Even the demons believe that—and shudder" (James 2:19).
- "You foolish person, do you want evidence that faith without deeds is useless?" (James 2:20).

- "You see that a person is considered righteous by what they do and not by faith alone" (James 2:24).
- "As the body without the spirit is dead, so faith without deeds is dead" (James 2:26).

The nature of true, saving faith is vital to understand, because it is the essential response to Jesus and the gospel.[41]

We want to make sure that we have saving faith, sealed by God. This faith can be defined in the following ways:

- *Saving faith is expressed in a decision and a commitment*—to trust and follow Jesus (Acts 2:38-39). By faith, we are given a new relationship with God, where we become disciples of Jesus. We commit to trust and follow Jesus through repentance, confession, and baptism.[42]
- *Saving faith is sealed by God's Spirit* (Ephesians 1:13-14). Walking with God, by the Spirit, is how the Bible describes our personal relationship with God (2 Corinthians 3:16-18). We responded to the Spirit at the time of salvation (1 John 2:20-27). After that, God is with us as we live a new life (Galatians 5:16-25). We know that someone is a Christian, saved and in relationship with God, by the indwelling Spirit (Romans 8:9,16).
- *Saving faith is to continue to trust and follow Jesus*—it is allegiance, loyalty, and faithfulness.[43] It is a commitment to be a disciple of Jesus. It leads to obedience. It involves continually seeking God and walking with him. False faith is content to live in sinful lifestyles (Galatians 5:19-21). False faith deliberately continues in sin (Hebrews 10:26-33). True faith means that we surrender our lives to be disciples of Jesus. It is a life of trusting and following God through Jesus.

This is the core message of the Bible. It calls us to make the decision to trust and follow Jesus. We become disciples of Jesus in response to the gospel. These elements are first bucket elements.

CHAPTER 8

Important Elements: The Second Bucket

Beyond the core truth of Jesus and his gospel, we find other elements of the faith. These are related to the essential gospel and are important, but secondary elements. Second-level elements are often truths that show us how to trust and follow Jesus, but these, in themselves, do not save us. Only Jesus Christ and active faith in his gospel can save. Secondary elements of the faith are important because all of God's truth is important. All truth can guide us in the way of Jesus as it protects, strengthens, and enables us to be faithful to God in various ways.

As we saw in the last chapter, the Bible makes it clear when an essential element is at stake. For example, as we saw in the last chapter, what Galatians 1:6-9 teaches about the gospel and what James 2:14-26 teaches on the nature of saving faith. Second bucket issues often require a more careful reading of the text.

Take 1 Corinthians as a model of the difference between the two buckets. The Apostle Paul writes this letter to deal with many problems. The Corinthian church is doing many things wrong. But he begins the letter by addressing them as people who are saved:

> To the church of God in Corinth, to those sanctified in Christ Jesus and called to be his holy people, together with all those everywhere who call on the name of our Lord Jesus Christ—their Lord and ours… For in him you have been enriched in every way—with all kinds of speech and with all knowledge—God thus confirming our testimony about Christ among you (1 Cor. 1:2-6).

As members of God's church in Corinth, we can know, in everything that follows, that they are "sanctified," "among those who call on the name of our Lord," "those enriched in every way," and those among whom "God is confirming the testimony about Christ." There is no doubt they are saved and heaven bound.

But carefully notice something: Paul corrects them and points out how their practices will dishonor God and harm people. These items are a big deal, even though *not essential to salvation*. He does not tell them that their status with God in eternity is in danger because of these issues. Here are seven samples from this letter, where they were "off" as a church:

- They had divisions and different camps in the church (1 Corinthians 1:10).
- They were caught up in worldly jealousy and quarreling (1 Corinthians 3:3).
- They were going beyond what the apostles had written in their practices (1 Corinthians 4:6).

- They were not bringing proper church discipline on a man who was sleeping with his father's wife (1 Corinthians 5:1-6).
- They were suing each other and taking each other to court (1 Corinthians 6:1-6).
- They were not acting properly in the way they took the Lord's Supper (1 Corinthians 11:17ff).
- They were not acting right with regard to spiritual gifts (1 Corinthians 12:1-13:13).

But in none of these areas does Paul tell them that they are lost over these items. He simply calls them to God's truth and to have a faithful faith.

By carefully reading 1 Corinthians and all the other New Testament books, we can see the cumulative case for important but not salvation truths. I (Bobby) have carefully examined every book in the New Testament with this filter. Salvation issues are treated much differently than important issues, as our short survey of 1 Corinthians, as a sample, has shown.

There are only two clear times in 1 Corinthians where the issues are salvation related. One is when Paul talks about a man actively living in sexual immorality with his father's wife (Chapter 5), and the second is when Paul talks about the gospel in 1 Corinthians 15.

Again, when it comes to the gospel, Paul is unyielding. He warns the Corinthians: "Now, brothers and sisters, I want to remind you of the gospel I preached to you, which you received and on which you have taken your stand. By this gospel you are saved, if you hold firmly to the word I preached to you. Otherwise, you have believed in vain" (1 Cor. 15:1-2). Notice here what Paul says about the gospel: 1) they have taken their stand on it, 2) they are saved by it, 3) they must hold firmly to it, and 4) otherwise they have believed in vain. These are strong words about their eternal destiny.

Paul also raises a concern about an essential matter for an individual (1 Cor. 5:1-2). Paul reprimands the church for allowing this man to be actively and sexually immoral, and then he tells the church that they must discipline the man by excluding him from the church. Paul tells these Christians to do this for the sake of the man. He describes the expulsion of the man and then what the discipline will bring about in the man's life: "Hand this man over to Satan for the destruction of the flesh, so that his spirit may be saved on the day of the Lord" (1 Cor. 5:5).

This man is living contrary to genuine faith. He is no longer living in the repentant posture that manifests true faith. In hopes that expelling the man will "turn him over to Satan for the destruction of the flesh," Paul hopes that this may cause him to repent and be saved. So, we see that unless it is the gospel itself or a lifestyle revealing that true faith no longer exists, one's salvation is secure.

When we are focused on the gospel and adhere to the path of discipleship by faith, we have a center point for our faith. This is the core teaching of the Bible, as we described in the last chapter. People who completely trust in Jesus and have committed themselves to the path of discipleship often disagree on these important biblical teachings. Don't miss this crucial point: we must not diminish biblical teaching just because it is not essential for salvation. That is not in step with true faith. It causes people to dishonor God, God's Word, God's wisdom, and the best path for humans, just to name a few of its effects. It also sets people up to lose critical thinking and cave in to the spirit of the age that minimizes truth. We must remember Hebrews 11:6 in all of these things: "Without faith it is impossible to please God, because anyone who comes to him must believe that he exists and that he rewards those who earnestly seek him." We want to seek God and God's way in all things.

We know that on many of these matters, God's truth will divide us into different churches. And as individuals, sometimes our convictions about biblical truth on these matters may mean we cannot "do church together." These are areas where the exercise of one person's faith causes the other person to violate their understanding of God's truth. For example, if a person believes that it is wrong for a church to appoint women elders or a woman lead pastor, then that person would violate their conscience to submit to such leadership. Or if the leadership of a church pushed the teaching of a modern-day prophet (as equal to Scripture), and a person believed that such a practice was not biblical or valid to that degree, then it would easily lead to conflicts of these important, secondary elements of the faith. Another example is ultimate individual predestination (Calvinism) versus free will. It would difficult for someone who believed in Calvinism to sit under the teaching of a church who believed in ultimate free will (Arminism). The biblical issues reflected in these two systems are important—and have important implications—but, in themselves, are not essential to salvation.

Here is a list of other important, second bucket truths:

- How a church tolerates sinful lifestyles of members (i.e., church discipline).
- How a church upholds a biblical conversion model.
- The leadership model of the local church: does it seek to have biblical and functional elders?
- Does the church push everyone to speak in tongues in the gatherings of the church as a sign of salvation?
- Do they teach that a person who turned away and abandoned Jesus could still be saved without repentance?
- How do they practice love as a church?
- Do they actively tolerate hatred, racism, or the like?
- Does the church seek to reach people who are eternally lost to fulfill the Great Commission?
- Does the church try to love the hurting and the poor?

- What do they teach about the grounds for divorce?
- What do they teach about gender roles in marriage?

On and on we can go. These are important differences that we take seriously, but they are secondary truths, and if someone is in error on one of these matters, they do not stop God's saving power and his adoption of us as his children. Even though these are matters of great concern, error on these points does not stop people in these churches from being Christians. Nor do they cause us to view those who hold these teachings differently than us as opponents or enemies. There are differences, but we have much more in common than in opposition. Our differences are between brothers and sisters who are bound by the Holy Spirit and Jesus' grace.

We know that on many of these matters God's truth will divide us into different churches. And, as individuals, we will need to hold to our convictions and we will not be able to attend churches where there are Christians who differ with us. It may be difficult, but convictions will require it. These are areas where the exercise of one person's faith causes the other person to violate their understanding and practice of God's truth.

One's inability to be in the same local church with someone is almost always because of differences in how we practice second level truths, not because of core-belief differences (the difference between *orthopraxy* versus *orthodoxy*). The gospel teaches us that we are all imperfect and struggling children who will *never get it all right* and who can only be saved by "grace through faith" (Eph. 2:8-9). So, we must often agree to disagree with our brothers and sisters and practice our faith differently. We are still united through our core faith in Jesus.

The last thing we want to address as we conclude this chapter comes in the light of all the pressures that people are facing in Western Civilization to be tolerant and accept differences without caring as much about truth. Simply put, we want to pursue God's truth to live under God's blessings. God's truth in Scripture is the best way for us to live. Psalm 19:8-11 describes all the ways we are blessed by following God's Word:

> The precepts of the Lord are right, giving joy to the heart. The commands of the Lord are radiant, giving light to the eyes. The fear of the Lord is pure, enduring forever. The decrees of the Lord are firm, and all of them are righteous. They are more precious than gold, than much pure gold; they are sweeter than honey, than honey from the honeycomb. By them your servant is warned; in keeping them there is great reward.

CHAPTER 9

Personal Elements: The Third Bucket

We are now at the outer ring, which our friend and Renew leader Douglas Jacoby calls the "peripheral elements of the faith."[44] We call them the personal elements of the faith or third bucket issues. What we mean by "personal" is that some truths or parts of the faith are almost impossible to have certainty on. They depend on the person or their situation or both.

When it comes to third bucket issues, we can almost always stay together in a local church. We function together because we agree on the gospel and on important but secondary elements of the faith. Yet on this third level of personal matters, where issues are less clear, God may not have a set path for all of us to follow. We learn to accept and respect our differences on these matters.

These "disputable matters" are described in Romans 14:2-4:

One person's faith allows them to eat anything, but another, whose faith is weak, eats only vegetables. The one who eats everything must not treat with contempt the one who does not, and the one who does not eat everything must not judge the one who does, for God has accepted them. Who are you to judge someone else's servant? To their own master, servants stand or fall. And they will stand, for the Lord is able to make them stand.

Some Christians in Rome ate pork, but others could not do so in good conscience because of their Jewish background. There was not a universal right or wrong on this; it was up to the individual person to work out with God. At this level, some Christians ate meat, some did not; some Christians drank wine, some did not.

We have such matters for Christians to figure out for themselves today. The Bible does not say that a practice is always right or always wrong, so God leaves it up to each of us to work out. The local church should do the same. For example:

- Some Christians go to R-rated movies, some do not.
- Some Christians drink wine (without getting drunk), some do not.
- Some Christians get tattoos, some do not.
- Some Christians date without chaperones, some never meet with the opposite sex alone.
- Some Christians will have an irregular cigar, some never use tobacco.

Many Christians struggle to wrap their minds around the reality of relative or personal truths. In their immaturity, they struggle. They want all things to be black and white. But at this third level, there is a consensus that clear biblical teaching on these issues does not exist.

We also believe that this same principle applies to hard-to-understand parts of the Bible that do not seem to impact the essential elements of the faith. For example, some Christians believe that the book of Revelation must be literal in most aspects and others do not. In areas like this, we can witness a unity-in-diversity. Again, each of these matters may be important to us as individuals, and in fact, the Bible teaches that at this level, we will still have to give an accounting of ourselves to God on some level (Rom. 14:10-12). But none of these matters determines our status as children of God, and we must be careful not to insist that our belief is the right one that must be bound on everyone else. Some of these matters are grey. We have great freedom of conscience to believe and practice what we think is best.

Here is another list of issues that fit into this category, as more examples for you to consider as you process this concept of the "third bucket":

- While accepting that Genesis 1-2 is the teaching of the infallible Word of God, some believe creation took place over millions of years and others believe it only took six literal days.
- Some believe the flood killed all humanity, who only lived in a restricted area on the earth, and others believe the flood covered the whole world.
- Some believe that the Bible prohibits instrumental music, and others believe it is authorized.
- Some believe that communion should be every week, and others believe it can be taken less often.

- Some believe that the rapture will come before a tribulation at the end of time, and some believe it will come at the end of tribulation.
- Some believe that women should wear head coverings in church, and some do not believe women need to have head coverings.

Many Christians are surprised to learn that there are relative and personal truths like these. At this third level, there is a consensus that explicit or clear biblical teachings are hard to find. In some cases, it clearly does not exist. For these, no clear teaching shows what is "right" or "wrong."

How do you feel when discussing items at each of these levels? When the gospel is at stake, it's easy to get emotionally charged up, like the Apostle Paul did in Galatians, for example. But what about these tertiary issues? Can we get charged up in discussions with people? We suggest not. While first bucket and second bucket issues can get more heated the closer you get to the gospel, we need to turn down the alarm and intensity of these third bucket issues.

The Bible teaches that we should not judge one another on these matters. Paul tells us what to do in Romans 14:10-13:

> You, then, why do you judge your brother or sister? Or why do you treat them with contempt? For we will all stand before God's judgment seat. It is written: "'As surely as I live,' says the Lord, 'every knee will bow before me; every tongue will acknowledge God.'" So then, each of us will give an account of ourselves to God. Therefore, let us stop passing judgment on one another. Instead, make up your mind not to put any stumbling block or obstacle in the way of a brother or sister.

So, the Bible teaches us to accept and not to judge those who make personal choices on what the Apostle Paul calls "disputable matters" (Rom. 14:1).

The whole point of the last four chapters has been to help us to think more critically about what issues and what truths we must prioritize in our conversations with each other as believers. When it comes to the Bible, we must remember the teachings of the earlier chapter—that everything is black and white… or sometimes grey. While the gospel is the core issue for us, many other teachings in the Bible come up!

Here are some recommendations to help us frame our mindset about conviction and civility:

- Our biggest concern should be that people know and have opportunity to respond to the gospel. Everything else takes the backseat compared to that.
- If someone holds to the gospel with a genuine faith, we should talk with and relate to them as a brother or sister. We will not get overly concerned about non-salvation issues, especially when we are involved with different churches, and we should try to work together on projects wherever possible.
- When God has made us brothers and sisters in Christ, it surely grieves him when we do not actively recognize one another. We should rejoice that we share the same faith in Jesus and the gospel. We like the slogan, "Christians only, but not the only Christians."
- We can accomplish many great things—and more effectively—in the cause of the gospel if we are united and working together with Christians in other churches—even those with whom we differ on important, second bucket matters.

- If we emphasize and show the world our unity in the gospel and our love for our brothers and sisters in other Christian fellowships, Scripture teaches that God will use it to help unbelievers see the truth of Christianity and come to believe (John 13:34-35; John 17:20-21).

CHAPTER 10

Final Thoughts

In a world where even Christians are becoming indifferent and, in some cases, opposed to Christian truth we must be ready to show our love for God and our love for others as Jesus did. The topics Jesus taught are counter-cultural and sometimes difficult to uphold. There is risk in the pursuit of truth and in our attempts to share it. We must balance the risk of being offensive by sharing convicted thought with our civil and "passionately polite" approach. We must do this while maintaining compassion that also builds deeper friendships and relationships.

We must balance our humble admission that we do not have all the answers with our preparedness to give reason for the hope that is in us in a substantive way. We must do all of this as we pray and trust that God's Spirit is at work. As we strive to achieve these balances, we must be sure we reach out to those who are different from us, as well.

With those challenges in mind, let's review our recommended approach of how we should discuss the truth with others today:

Practice Convicted Civility

- Too many people who are good at being civil lack strong convictions, and too many people who have strong convictions lack civility. We suggest "convicted civility."
- We are called to show gentleness and respect.
- We must pursue empathy and genuine curiosity of others.
- We should be humble and teachable in discussions with others.
- In Christ, we should maintain a passionate, yet polite, conviction about the truth of Scripture.

Pursue Relational Discipleship

- Relational discipleship begins at "hello" and can lead to a strong relational foundation for having hard conversations.
- Good relationships are the best way to share truth.
- In the context of personal relationships, we can ask questions, explain nuances, and share real-life examples.
- Love is the way of Jesus who told us to love others "as I have loved you."

Uphold Critical Thinking

- A key aspect of loving God is to love him with our minds.
- This means sharing what we believe about our faith.
- Everybody who has thoughts about God is a theologian, and we should be substantive and responsible theologians.

Acknowledge that Everything is Black and White... or Grey

- In life and in the Bible, some things are clear and essential.
- In life and in the Bible, some things that are clear are also important.
- In life and in the Bible, many things are grey, relative, or unclear.

Guard Against Defensiveness

- Begin active improvement of your own emotional health before discipling others.
- Determine in advance what elements are worth dividing over and why.

Develop a Clear Understanding of the Elements of Biblical Faith (a.k.a. the "Three Buckets")

- Seek to understand and prepare a defense of those biblical elements which are essential.
- Determine the elements that are important and make the decision to take a stand for them.
- Remember God gives freedom in many areas where things are not right or wrong. There are teachings you will feel are morally and personally true for you, but we must not cause our brothers and sisters to stumble with our choices on these.

Remember Love in all Things

In the *Disciple Maker's Handbook,* Bobby and Josh Patrick shared a summary about dealing with people.[45] We feel it is an appropriate thought to close with. It went something like this…

Confused about the "Christian response" to hard issues? Use this reference list:

Male – love them.
Female – love them.
Unsure – love them.
Gay – love them.
Straight – love them.
Unsure – love them.
Addict – love them.
Sober – love them.

Believer – love them.
Unbeliever – love them.
Unsure – love them.

We can summarize everything with one word: love. We want to love God and the truths of his Word. We also want to love people the way God teaches us. In the end, love is our entire goal.

Endnotes

1. Dallas Willard, *The Allure of Gentleness: Defending the Faith in the Manner of Jesus* (San Francisco, Cal.: Harper One, 2015).
2. Ibid., 4.
3. Richard J. Mouw, *Uncommon Decency*, second ed. (Downers Grove, Ill.: InterVarsity Press, 2010), 14.
4. Ibid., 13.
5. Ibid., 20.
6. Ibid., 32.
7. Ibid., 58.
8. Ibid., 59.
9. Ibid., 60.
10. Ibid., 61.
11. Ibid., 62.
12. Lee Strobel, *The Case for Faith* (Grand Rapids, Mich.: Zondervan, 2000), 32.
13. David Kinnaman and Gabe Lyons, *Good Faith* (Ada, MI: Baker Books, 2016), 13.
14. Ibid., 13.
15. The study is from Cornell University: Caitlin Dewey, "How to win a Facebook argument, according to science," *The Washington Post*, Feb. 11, 2016, https://arxiv.org/pdf/1602.01103v1.pdf.
16. Minda Zetlin, "You Should Never, Ever Argue With Anyone on Facebook, According to Science," Inc.com, Nov. 29,

2017, https://www.inc.com/minda-zetlin/you-should-never-
ever-argue-with-anyone-on-facebook-according-to-science.
html.

17. Kinnaman and Lyons, *Good Faith*, 162.

18. Ibid., 162.

19. Bobby Harrington and Josh Patrick, *The Disciple Maker's Handbook* (Grand Rapids, MI: Zondervan, 2017), 64.

20. Kinnaman and Lyons, *Good Faith*, 81.

21. Carla Hinton, "Authors discuss how to share 'Good Faith'," newsok.com, Feb. 10, 2017, https://newsok.com/article/5537689/authors-discuss-how-to-share-good-faith.

22. Harrington and Patrick, *The Disciple Maker's Handbook*, 51.

23. Matthew 22:36-40.

24. John Piper, *Think: The Life of the Mind and the Love of God* (Chicago, IL: Crossway, 2010), 83.

25. 1 Peter 3:15.

26. Ravi Zacharias, "Indispensable Apologetics: An Interview with Ravi Zacharias," *Tabletalk Magazine*, Aug. 1, 2012, https://www.ligonier.org/learn/articles/indispensable-apologetics/.

27. Amy B. Wang, "'Post-truth' named 2016 word of the year by Oxford Dictionaries," *The Washington Post*, last updated November 8, 2016, https://www.washingtonpost.com/news/the-fix/wp/2016/11/16/post-truth-named-2016-word-of-the-year-by-oxford-dictionaries/?utm_term=.0ab602fddbc9/.

28. We recommend those who want to go deeper become familiar with Thomas Oden, Bernard Lonergan, C.S. Lewis, William Lane Craig, and Alvin Plantinga.

29. Bernard Lonergan, *Method in Theology, 2nd ed.* (Toronto, Ont.: University of Toronto Press, 1990).

30. Mark Ross, "In Essentials Unity, In Non Essentials Liberty, In all thing Charity," accessed September 28, 2018, https://www.ligonier.org/learn/articles/essentials-unity-non-essentials-liberty-all-things/.

31. You can find out more about Pete's ministry by going to https://www.emotionallyhealthy.org/.

32. The following material is taken from the book by Bobby Harrington, *How to Trust and Follow Jesus: A Study Guide* (2017), 14.

33. Bobby Harrington owns the image rights to all images in the text of this book.

34. We are grateful for several scholars whose work on the gospel has helped us; we especially commend the extensive work on the New Testament teaching on the gospel in Matthew Bates's forthcoming book, which we have been able to preview, *Gospel Allegiance* (Ada, MI: Brazos, 2019).

35. For an in-depth study on the New Testament meaning of faith, see Matthew Bates, *Salvation by Allegiance Alone: Rethinking Faith, Works, and the Gospel of Jesus the King* (Ada, MI: Baker Academic, 2017).

36. For more on this definition of a disciple, see Discipleship.org, and Jim Putman and Bobby Harrington *DiscipleShift* (Grand Rapids: Zondervan, 2013).

37. Parts of this statement are drawn from and adapted from "The Gospel of Jesus Christ: An Evangelical Celebration," copyright 1999 by the Committee on Evangelical Unity in the Gospel, P.O. Box 5551, Glendale Heights, IL, 60139-5551, which was first published in *Christianity Today* (August, 1999).

38. Ibid.

39. Matthew Bates devotes a significant time to this correlation in his book, *Salvation by Allegiance Alone: Rethinking Faith, Works, and the Gospel of Jesus the King* (Ada, MI: Baker Academic, 2017).

40. We're not saying God can't save those from these Christian groups, but when he does, it will be the result of people finding the true gospel—and in most cases, it will be in spite of what these groups teach about it.

41. Robert Picirilli does a great job of showing how the emphasis that we are saved "by grace through faith" and discipleship coalesce. *Discipleship: The Expression of Saving Faith* (Nashville: Randall House, 2013).

42. For further study on this topic, we recommend a fee eBook that I (Bobby) wrote with others called, *Baptism: What the Bible Teaches* (see Renew.org).

43. See Matthew Bates, *Salvation by Allegiance Alone: Rethinking Faith, Works, and the Gospel of Jesus the King* (Ada, MI: Baker Academic, 2017).

44. See more of Douglas Jacoby's similar perspective by going to https://www.douglasjacoby.com/.

45. Harrington and Patrick, *The Disciple Maker's Handbook*, 67.

About the Authors

JASON HENDERSON has spent over 20 years in corporate leadership. His experience includes Fortune 500, military and both public and private organizations. He has led professionally on governing boards, in corporate associations and in over 30 countries. He is the COO for Renew.org and a team member of Discipleship.org. He is a graduate of Virginia Tech and the Culinary Institute of America. He lives in Franklin, Tennessee, with his wife and two children.

BOBBY HARRINGTON is a co-founder and the executive director of Renew. He has completed graduate work in diverse places like the University of Calgary, Harding University, Princeton Seminary, and Regent College. He also holds a Doctorate of Ministry from Southern Baptist Theological Seminary. He is the founding and lead pastor of Harpeth Christian Church, the former director of research and development in missional leadership for Stadia, a co-founder of the Relational Discipleship Network, and the co-founder and executive director of Discipleship.org. He is also the author or co-author of over ten books on disciple making, including *DiscipleShift* and *The Disciple Maker's Handbook*. He is married to Cindy, and they have two married children and two grandchildren.

www.ingramcontent.com/pod-product-compliance
Lightning Source LLC
Chambersburg PA
CBHW060719030426
42337CB00017B/2928